THE LEE F. SIMMONS STORY

THE LEE F. SIMMONS STORY

AMERICA'S FIRST AFRICAN-AMERICAN AIR FORCE ONE STEWARD

Victor Simmons

To purchase books in bulk, please contact the publisher.

Mynd Matters Publishing
2690 Cobb Parkway SE
Ste A5-375
Smyrna, GA 30080
www.myndmatterspublishing.com

978-1-963874-84-6 (pbk)
978-1-963874-85-3 (hdcv)
978-1-963874-86-0 (e-ISBN)

FIRST EDITION

For my father, Lee F. Simmons,
who showed the world that presence,
not position, creates lasting influence.
And for his grandchildren, great-
grandchildren, and every child who
dreams of flying high.

Contents

Chapter 1

In 1931, in a tiny wooden shack in Nymph, Alabama, a very special baby was born. His name was Lee Fonzie Simmons, and he would be the first of nine children.

The humble homestead was so small that you could barely fit his grandparents and all of his siblings. It had no running water, which meant no faucets or toilets. It had no electricity, which meant no light switches or lamps. But even though their home was small and simple, it was filled with something much more important than fancy things.

It was filled with LOVE.

Lee's grandparents, Bill and Ella Belle Simmons, took care of him on their farm. Grandfather Bill was strong and quiet, with hands that could fix anything. Grandmother Ella Belle had a warm smile and a voice that could make anyone feel better, especially when she sang hymns while working around the house.

Every morning before the sun came up, Lee would wake to the sound of roosters crowing. His first job was to help with the farm chores. He fed the chickens, gathered warm eggs from their nests, and helped water the many plants that grew on their land.

The farm had rows and rows of corn that grew tall as grown-ups. There were tomato plants heavy with red fruit, peach trees that smelled sweet in the summer, and even sugar cane that made everything taste good. Lee learned to take care of them all.

But Lee's very best friend on the farm was Roadie, the mule. Roadie was brown with big, gentle eyes and ears that flopped when he walked. Every day, Roadie helped pull the plow through the fields and carry heavy loads around the farm. When Lee finished his chores, he would pat Roadie's neck and sometimes share an apple with his four-legged friend.

"Lee," his grandmother would say as she

watched him with Roadie, "remember to work hard, be kind to everyone, and always do your best. Those are the most important things in life."

"Yes, ma'am," Lee would answer, not knowing that those simple words would one day shape the kind of leader he would become.

The farm kept everyone busy. Lee's grandfather made sure there was always food on the table and a roof over their heads. His grandmother, the local midwife, helped bring babies into the world, and she taught Lee that helping others was one of life's greatest gifts.

Even though they didn't have much money, the Simmons family was wealthy in the things that really mattered: love, hard work, and dreams for the future.

Little Lee had no idea that the boy who carried water buckets from the stream and helped his friend Roadie would grow up to work on the most famous airplane in the whole world—Air Force One, the U.S. President's plane!

Chapter 2

When Lee was fourteen, something exciting happened that would change his life forever. One hot summer day, a shiny blue Cadillac came driving up the dusty road to the farm. The car was so beautiful it looked like it belonged in a magazine!

Out stepped a tall, well-dressed man with a big smile and confident walk. Lee had never seen anyone quite like him.

"Lee," said his grandfather, "I'd like you to meet Willie Fate Simmons. This is your father."

Lee's eyes grew wide. His father! Willie Fate walked over with his arms open wide.

"Well, look at you, son!" Willie Fate said, his voice warm and friendly. "You've grown into a fine young man. How would you like to come live with me in Akron, Ohio? There's a whole world waiting for you up there!"

Lee looked at his grandparents, who nodded encouragingly.

"It would be good for you, Lee," his grandmother said. "You can finish high school there and learn about your father's business."

So, Lee packed his few belongings and said goodbye to his grandparents, Roadie, and the farm. As they drove away in that beautiful Cadillac, Lee watched the small homestead get smaller and smaller until it disappeared behind the trees.

In Akron, Ohio, Lee discovered that his father was quite a remarkable man. Willie Fate owned a catering business, which meant he prepared and served food for parties and special events. He could talk to anyone—rich people, poor people, important people—and make them all feel like his best friend.

"Son," Willie Fate said on Lee's first day in the big city, "in this business, it's not just about the food. It's about making people feel special. When you serve someone, you're showing them respect."

Lee watched his father work and was

amazed. Willie Fate could remember exactly how each customer liked their coffee. He knew just the right words to make people smile. He could arrange flowers on a table and make them look like art.

"Let me teach you," Willie Fate said, handing Lee a white apron. "First lesson: everything must be perfect. The plates must shine. The glasses must sparkle. When people see our work, they should say, 'Wow!'"

Lee learned to polish silver until he could see his reflection. He practiced folding napkins into perfect triangles. He learned to walk smoothly while carrying a tray, even on uneven floors.

But the most important lesson came when Willie Fate took him to serve at a fancy party.

"Remember, Lee," his father whispered as they approached the grand house, "every person who walks through that door is important. Greet them with a smile. Make them feel welcome. That's the secret to success in life."

At the party, Lee watched his father work

like magic. "Good evening, Mrs. Peterson! How lovely you look tonight!" "Mr. Johnson, I saved you a piece of that chocolate cake you enjoyed so much last time!"

Everyone loved Willie Fate. They would seek him out just to talk and laugh. Lee began to understand that his father wasn't just serving food—he was serving kindness.

"Why do you treat everyone so special?" Lee asked on the drive home.

Willie Fate pulled the car over and looked at his son.

"Lee, I learned something important growing up. It doesn't matter if someone is rich or poor, famous or unknown. Every person deserves to be treated with respect. When you make someone feel valued, you're giving them a gift that costs nothing but means everything."

Lee nodded, storing the wisdom in his heart.

Week after week, Lee worked alongside his father. He learned everything about his catering business from buying the food to serving it to how to make a profit and most importantly, to care for people. He didn't know it then, but every lesson, every smile, every "yes, sir" and "yes, ma'am" was preparing him for something extraordinary.

One day, Lee would use these exact same skills to welcome kings and queens, presidents and prime ministers aboard the most important airplane in America. But that was still a dream waiting to unfold.

For now, Lee was just a young man learning from his father that the secret to a good life was simple: work hard, treat people well, and always, always serve with your heart.

Chapter 3

When Lee grew up, he knew he wanted to serve his country. After finishing his education and working with his father's catering business, Lee made an important decision. He walked into the Air Force recruitment office in Akron and raised his right hand to take an oath.

"I want to be the best airman I can be," Lee told himself as he looked at his reflection wearing his crisp blue uniform for the first time. The uniform made him stand taller and feel prouder than he ever had before.

Air Force training was the hardest thing Lee had ever done! Every morning, the drill sergeant's whistle blew at dawn. "Rise and shine, recruits! Today we separate the strong from the weak!"

Lee had to wake up earlier than he ever had on the farm. He had to run farther than he ever had in Alabama. He had to follow orders faster and more precisely than anything his father had taught him in the catering business.

Some days, Lee's muscles ached so much he could barely move. Some nights, he was so tired he fell asleep the moment his head hit the pillow. But he remembered what his grandfather had taught him about working hard and never giving up.

"This is making me stronger," Lee would tell himself during the toughest moments.

"Every push-up, every mile I run, every order I follow is preparing me for something important."

The Air Force taught Lee many things. He learned to march in perfect formation with his fellow airmen. He learned to keep his uniform spotless and his shoes so shiny they looked like mirrors. He learned about discipline, teamwork, and what it meant to serve something bigger than yourself.

Lee was assigned to work as a mail courier, delivering important letters and packages around the Air Force base. As he walked through the offices in his sharp uniform, people began to notice something special about him. He was very good at handling the many situations that confronted him in his duties with calm and grace. He was always helpful when someone needed assistance. And you could tell he simply enjoyed people and learned to be comfortable with himself.

"Good morning, Sergeant Lee!" officers would call out as he passed by. "How are you today?"

"Very well, sir, thank you for asking," Lee would reply, snapping a crisp salute. "Is there anything I can help you with?"

The other airmen began to see that Lee had a gift for making people feel comfortable and welcome. Whether he was delivering mail to a general or helping a new recruit find his way around the base, Lee treated everyone with the same respect and kindness his father had taught him.

Lee's skills as an airman continued to grow. He learned how to take care of important people when they traveled on Air Force planes. His job was to make sure passengers were comfortable, their food was served properly, and they felt safe during their flights. The Air Force recognized his talents and gave him more essential responsibilities. Soon after Lee's efforts paid off, he received exciting news: he was being reassigned to Rhine-Main Air Force Base in Frankfurt, Germany! He would serve as Chief Steward, flying with the United States Air Force Commanding Chief of Europe.

For two years, Lee flew all over Europe, taking care of high-ranking military leaders. He learned about different countries and cultures. He practiced the lessons his father had taught him about making every person feel special, whether they were from America, Germany, France, or anywhere else in the world.

Lee was exceptional at his job. He could handle any situation that came up during flights with calm and grace. The pilots trusted him. The passengers appreciated his kindness. And most importantly, Lee was becoming known throughout the Air Force as someone very special.

Then one day, something incredible happened. The telephone rang in Lee's quarters in Germany. On the other end was Colonel Ralph Albertazzi, the personal pilot to the President of the United States and Commander of the most important airplane in the world.

"Sergeant Simmons," the Colonel said, "I've been watching your work, and I've heard wonderful things about you from everyone who has flown with you. I have a very important question to ask you."

Lee's heart began to beat faster.

"I would like to personally request that you return to the United States to fly on Air Force One as a steward. You would be serving the President of the United States. Would you be interested in this position?"

Lee could hardly believe what he was hearing. Air Force One! The President's airplane! Colonel Albertazzi, the most important pilot in the Air Force, was personally asking for him!

"Yes, sir!" Lee answered without hesitation. "I would be deeply honored to serve."

Chapter 4

After Colonel Albertazzi's phone call, Lee's whole world changed. He was going to serve aboard Air Force One, the President's airplane! No Black person had ever been chosen for this job before. Lee would be making history.

The next few weeks were a whirlwind of activity. Lee had to pack up his life in Germany and prepare to move back to the United States with his wife, Jeannette, and their children, two toddlers and a newborn. But most importantly, he had to prepare for the biggest responsibility of his life.

When Lee arrived at Andrews Air Force Base in Maryland, he could hardly believe his eyes. There, sitting on the tarmac like a magnificent blue and white jewel, was Air Force One.

The airplane was enormous! It was much

larger than any plane Lee had ever seen. The beautiful blue paint gleamed in the sunlight, and UNITED STATES OF AMERICA was painted in bold letters along the side. At the front of the plane was the presidential seal, a symbol that told the whole world that the most powerful person in America traveled on this aircraft.

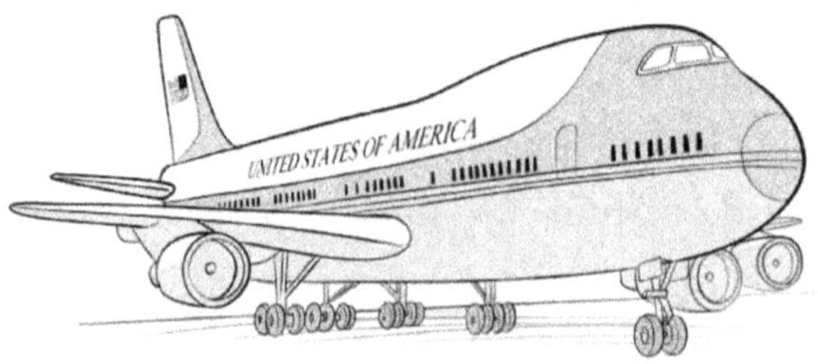

“Welcome to Air Force One, Sergeant Simmons,” said Colonel Albertazzi as he greeted Lee at the base of the airplane steps. “Are you ready to see what will be your new office?”

“Yes, sir!” Lee replied, trying to contain his excitement.

As they climbed the steps and entered the

plane, Lee felt like he was stepping into a flying palace. The inside of Air Force One was unlike anything he had ever imagined. There were beautiful leather seats, polished wood tables, and carpets so thick and soft they felt like walking on clouds.

"This is the presidential suite," Colonel Albertazzi explained, showing Lee a spacious room with a large desk, comfortable chairs, and even a bed. "This is where the President works and rests during long flights."

They walked through a conference room with a massive table where the President could meet with advisors. There was a communications center filled with telephones and radios that could reach anywhere in the world. There was even a medical room in case anyone got sick during a flight.

"And this," said Colonel Albertazzi, opening a door to a gleaming kitchen, "is where you'll prepare meals and take care of our passengers. Your job, Sergeant Simmons, is to make sure every person who steps aboard this aircraft feels welcome and comfortable."

Lee looked around the kitchen with its shining surfaces and modern equipment. He thought about his father's catering business and all the lessons he had learned about making people feel special.

"I understand, sir," Lee said. "Every person who comes aboard will be treated with respect and kindness."

"That's exactly right," Colonel Albertazzi smiled. "But Lee, I want you to understand something very important. You're not just serving any passengers. You'll be serving the President of the United States, foreign leaders, generals, senators, and some of the most powerful people in the world."

Lee's heartbeat quickened as he thought about meeting such important people.

"More than that," the Colonel continued, "you'll often be the first person these visitors see when they board Air Force One. You'll be standing at that door, welcoming them aboard. You'll represent not just this airplane, not just the Air Force, but America itself."

Lee stood a little taller as he realized the

importance of what Colonel Albertazzi was telling him.

"Do you think you're ready for that responsibility?" the Colonel asked.

Lee thought about his grandfather's farm in Alabama, where he learned that hard work and kindness could overcome any challenge. He thought about his father in Ohio, who taught him that every person deserves to be treated with respect. He thought about his training in the Air Force, where he learned about service and duty.

"Yes, sir," Lee said with confidence. "I'm ready to serve my country and make everyone who flies on Air Force One feel welcome."

Colonel Albertazzi shook Lee's hand firmly. "I believe you are, son. I believe you are."

Over the next few weeks, Lee trained with the other stewards on Air Force One. He learned where everything was stored, how all the equipment worked, and what the President liked for his meals. He practiced walking through the airplane smoothly, even when it was bumpy in the air. He learned the names and preferences of the people who traveled regularly with the President.

Lee's first missions included flights with Mrs. Kennedy and backup planes for President Kennedy. But even though Lee was now serving on the most important aircraft in America, he quickly learned that not everything would be easy. When they traveled through some cities in the southern states, the old segregation rules still existed. While the other crew members could stay in the same hotel together, Lee had to find different places to stay because of his race.

It was difficult and unfair, but Lee remembered his grandfather's lessons about perseverance and his father's teachings about maintaining dignity no matter what. He focused on doing his job with excellence, knowing that his service was slowly helping change the world for the better.

Lee practiced what would become his signature: standing at the door of Air Force One with a warm, welcoming smile, ready to greet whoever was about to step aboard the most famous airplane in the world.

"Welcome to Air Force One!" he would say, and every person who heard those words from Lee felt like they were the most important passenger on the plane.

Soon, Lee would meet Presidents and kings, generals and ambassadors. He would fly to countries he had only read about in books. He would witness history being made at 30,000 feet.

Chapter 5

Lee's most memorable mission aboard Air Force One was both exciting and sad. It was November 22, 1963, and President John F. Kennedy had been shot and killed in Dallas, Texas. The whole country was in shock and mourning.

Lee watched with a heavy heart as Air Force One landed in Dallas to bring President Kennedy home one last time. It was not the kind of mission anyone would want, but Lee knew he had an important job to do during this difficult time for America.

On that same flight, aboard Air Force One, something historic happened. Vice President Lyndon Johnson was sworn in as the new President of the United States. Lee stood quietly nearby as Judge Sarah Hughes raised her right hand and administered the oath of office. It was the first time a woman judge had ever sworn in a U.S. President.

Even during this tragic time, Lee did his job with grace and dignity, making sure everyone aboard was taken care of during the long, sorrowful flight back to Washington.

As the months and years passed, Lee's job became more familiar, but it never stopped being amazing. Because of his excellent work and the trust he had earned from everyone aboard Air Force One, Lee was promoted to

Chief Steward during the Nixon administration. This meant he was now in charge of all the other stewards and responsible for making sure everything ran perfectly on every flight.

His primary duty was still to stand at the door of Air Force One and welcome every person who came aboard.

"Welcome to Air Force One!" Lee would say with his warm, genuine smile. Whether it was a senator, a general, a foreign ambassador, or even a king or queen, Lee made each person feel like they were the most important passenger on the plane.

Lee served four different Presidents during his time on Air Force One: President Kennedy, President Johnson, President Nixon, and President Ford. Each President was different, but Lee treated them all with the same respect and kindness his father had taught him in the catering business.

President Johnson was a big man with a big personality who loved to talk. President Nixon was quieter and serious, always thinking about important decisions. President Ford was friendly and down-to-earth, treating everyone like they were part of his family.

But Lee's most exciting missions were the historic trips that changed the world. In February 1972, Lee flew with President Nixon on a trip that no American President had ever made before—to China! For many years, America and China had not been friends, but President Nixon wanted to change that.

As Air Force One landed in Beijing, Lee looked out the window at a country he had only heard about in stories. The Chinese people had never seen the American President's airplane before, and they were just as curious about Air Force One as Lee was about their country.

During the trip, Lee met Chinese officials and saw how President Nixon and the Chinese leaders worked together to become friends. Lee realized he was witnessing history being made.

"This is incredible," Lee thought to himself as he served tea to President Nixon and the Chinese premier. *A boy from Alabama is helping the President of the United States make peace with a country on the other side of the world!*

A few months later, Lee flew with President Nixon to Moscow, Russia, for another historic meeting. Russia and America had been enemies during something called the Cold War, but President Nixon wanted to find ways for the two countries to get along better.

Lee watched as President Nixon met with the Russian leader, Leonid Brezhnev. They signed important agreements that helped make the world a safer place. Once again, Lee was there to witness history.

Throughout all these missions, Lee met some of the most famous and powerful people in the world. He served meals to Henry Kissinger, the Secretary of State, who was known for his brilliant mind. He welcomed foreign presidents and prime ministers from countries all around the globe.

But no matter how famous or important the passengers were, Lee always remembered his father's most important lesson: treat every person with respect and kindness. Whether he was serving the President of the United States or helping a staff member find their seat, Lee made everyone feel valued.

The other crew members noticed how special Lee was at his job. The pilots trusted him completely. The Secret Service agents respected him. And most importantly, every President he served came to rely on Lee's calm, friendly presence.

"Lee has a gift," Colonel Albertazzi once said. "He can make anyone feel comfortable and welcome. That's exactly what we need on Air Force One."

Lee flew on hundreds of missions during his years on Air Force One. He traveled to countries he had never dreamed of visiting: Egypt, Japan, Germany, France, Italy, and many others. He saw the pyramids in Egypt, famous castles in Europe, and beautiful temples in Asia.

But the most rewarding part of his job wasn't the places he went or the famous people he met. It was knowing that every day, he was serving his country and representing America to the world.

Every time Lee stood at that airplane door and said, "Welcome to Air Force One," he was showing the world that America was a place where a boy from a small homestead in Alabama could grow up to serve Presidents and help make history. And that made Lee very proud indeed.

Chapter 6

In 1976, something sad happened for President Ford but wonderful for Lee. President Ford lost his reelection to Jimmy Carter, which meant Ford would no longer be President. For most people, this would mean the end of their work together. But President Ford had a very special request for Lee.

One morning, Lee received a message that President Ford wanted to see him in the Oval Office. Lee had been to the famous round office many times, but he had never been called there for a private meeting with the President.

"Come in, Lee," President Ford said warmly as Lee entered the most important office in America. "Please, have a seat. I have something very important to ask you."

Lee sat down in one of the comfortable chairs, wondering what the President could want to discuss with him.

"Lee," President Ford began, "in a few weeks, I'll be leaving the White House and moving to California to begin my life as a former President. I'll be serving on several important boards and working on my presidential library in Michigan."

Lee nodded, listening carefully.

"I'm going to need a personal assistant to help me with all of these new responsibilities," President Ford continued. "Someone I can trust completely. Someone who knows how to take care of important details. Someone who understands how to work with all kinds of people."

President Ford looked directly at Lee with a smile.

"Lee, I can't think of anyone I'd rather have by my side than you. Would you consider leaving the Air Force and coming to work for me personally in California?"

Lee was amazed! A former President was asking him to become part of his personal staff. This was an incredible honor.

"Mr. President," Lee replied, "I would be deeply honored to continue serving you."

"Wonderful!" President Ford said, shaking Lee's hand. "This means you'll need to move your family to California, and you'll be retiring from the Air Force after many years of distinguished service. But I promise you, we'll have many more adventures together."

A few months later, Lee and his family packed up their belongings and moved to the sunny Coachella Valley in California, settling in Palm Desert. Lee had traded his Air Force uniform for civilian clothes, but his mission remained the same: serving others with excellence and dedication.

Working for former President Ford was different from flying on Air Force One, but it was just as important. Lee helped President Ford prepare for board meetings, arranged his travel to speaking engagements around the country, and assisted with the planning of the Gerald R. Ford Presidential Library in Michigan.

But the best part of Lee's new job was getting to know President Ford not just as the leader of the free world, but as a regular person. They traveled together frequently, and Lee saw how kind and down-to-earth President Ford really was.

On one trip overseas, they were attending a formal dinner. Before the meal began, President Ford got up to speak with someone, and Lee stood behind his chair waiting. Someone came and sat in Lee's seat. Surprised but polite, Lee simply moved to the next chair. Then someone took that seat too! Lee moved once more, ending up three seats away from where he started.

When President Ford returned and saw Lee sitting so far away, he asked, “Lee, why did you move?”

Lee realized he could have politely told the first person that it was his seat, but his humble nature had made him just keep moving rather than cause any trouble. President Ford’s question helped Lee understand that sometimes it’s okay to speak up for yourself while still being kind to others.

Lee worked with President Ford for over thirty years! Even after President Ford’s death, Lee continued to help Mrs. Betty Ford until she no longer needed his assistance.

During all those years in California, Lee didn’t just work, he also gave back to his community. He volunteered with the Boys and Girls Club, helping young people just like his own grandparents had helped him. He served on community boards and always looked for ways to make life better for others.

Lee had learned that true success wasn’t just about the important job you held or the famous people you knew. It was about using your abilities to help others and make the world a little bit better.

For all his years of faithful service, Lee received many medals and honors: the Presidential Service Badge, the Air Force Commendation Medal, the Presidential Service Certificate, the Order of the New China Hands, the Moscow Summit Certificate, and the Meritorious Service Medal. He also received a special Certificate of Appreciation from Mrs. Pat Nixon.

But the greatest reward wasn't the medals or the recognition. It was knowing that a little boy from a homestead in Alabama had grown up to serve his country with honor, work alongside Presidents, and show the world that with hard work, kindness, and determination, any dream can come true.

Lee had traveled from a small homestead to Air Force One to the sunny valleys of California, but the most important journey had been the one in his heart—learning to serve others and make a difference in the world.

Chapter 7

Years passed, and Lee continued to serve with the same warm heart and strong work ethic his grandparents had taught him on that little homestead in Alabama. He had traveled around the world, met kings and queens, and worked alongside four U.S. presidents.

People from everywhere knew Lee Simmons. Presidents trusted him. World leaders smiled when they saw him. Children in his community looked up to him as a hero. But Lee never forgot where he came from or the simple lessons that had guided him throughout his life.

One day, a young boy in California approached Lee at a community event.

"Mr. Simmons," the boy asked with wide, curious eyes, "how did you do it? How did you get from that little homestead in Alabama all the way to Air Force One?"

Lee smiled the same warm smile he had been sharing his whole life. He knelt down so he could look the boy in the eyes, just like his grandfather used to do with him.

"Well," Lee said thoughtfully, "my grandparents taught me three very important things when I was about your age. First, always work hard, no matter what job you're doing. Second, be kind to everyone you meet, because every person is important. And third, never give up on your dreams, even when things seem impossible."

The boy listened carefully as Lee continued.

"My father taught me that when you serve other people, you're not just doing a job, you're showing them respect and making them feel valued. The Air Force taught me that serving your country is one of the greatest honors in life."

"But most importantly," Lee said, "I learned that it doesn't matter where you start in life. What matters is how you treat people, how hard you're willing to work, and whether you use your abilities to help others."

The little boy's eyes grew even wider. "So, anyone can achieve their dreams?"

"Anyone," Lee said with certainty. "If a little boy from Nymph, Alabama, who used to carry water buckets from a stream and help a mule named Roadie can grow up to serve Presidents, then any child with a dream and the willingness to work for it can achieve amazing things."

Lee looked around at all the children gathered at the community center. Some of them reminded him of himself when he was young. Maybe they felt like their dreams were too big, or their beginnings were too small.

"The secret is remembering that every person you meet is important. Whether you're serving the President of the United States or helping a friend with their homework, treat them with the same kindness and respect. That's what really matters."

As Lee stood, he thought about his incredible journey. From that tiny homestead in Alabama to the most famous airplane in the world. From carrying water buckets to serving Presidents. From a boy who had so little to a man who had given so much.

He had learned that being the first African American steward on Air Force One wasn't just about breaking barriers for himself. It was about showing others that they could dream big dreams too.

He thought about his grandfather Bill, who worked so hard on that farm and taught him that honest work had dignity. He thought about his grandmother Ella Belle, who showed him the importance of kindness and helping others. He thought about his mother,

Darnella, who wrapped her family in love but could be tough when they stepped out of line, teaching him that discipline was a form of love, too. He thought about his father Willie Fate, who taught him that every person deserves to be treated with respect.

All of their lessons had led him on this amazing journey.

Lee Simmons had shown the world that with determination, kindness, and hard work, any dream, no matter how big, can come true. He had proven that where you come from doesn't determine where you can go.

And somewhere in Alabama, if you listen closely on a quiet evening, you might still hear the echo of his grandmother's words floating on the breeze: "Work hard, be kind to everyone, and always do your best."

Those simple words from a small homestead had carried a little boy all the way to the sky, where he flew with Presidents and helped make history.

Lee's dream had come true. And now it was time for other children to start dreaming their own big dreams.

Author's Note

Lee F. Simmons (1931-2018) truly was the first African American steward to serve aboard Air Force One. His remarkable journey from humble beginnings in rural Alabama to serving four U.S. Presidents demonstrates the power of character, determination, and service to others.

This book is based on Mr. Simmons' own words about his life and service, as well as historical records. His story teaches us that success comes not from where you start, but from how you treat others and how hard you work toward your goals.

Lee's legacy reminds us that breaking barriers isn't just about personal achievement. It's about opening doors for others to follow their dreams, too.

About the Author

Victor Simmons is the eldest son of Lee and Jeannette Simmons. Growing up in a household shaped by his father's service aboard Air Force One and his mother's boundless creativity, Victor experienced firsthand the lessons of discipline, hospitality, and resilience that defined the Simmons family.

As a child, he listened to stories of world travels and presidential service, but also learned the importance of responsibility through Saturday morning chores, pancake breakfasts, and a home that always had room for one more. These memories form the foundation of *Life Lessons from Air Force One: Growing Up Simmons.*

Professionally, Victor built a career that mirrors the values instilled by his parents. He rose to senior leadership roles in human resources and organizational culture within the hospitality industry, guiding teams across the United States and abroad. He also became a recognized voice in diversity, equity, inclusion, and belonging (DEIB)—a natural extension of his father's example of service and dignity, and his mother's tenacity and the gift of curiosity.

Today, Victor continues that legacy as a speaker, consultant, and coach. Through his company, Victorious Endeavors, he helps leaders and organizations create cultures where people can thrive. His writing and storytelling carry forward the Simmons family tradition: blending discipline with compassion, excellence with humility, and service with love.

www.ingramcontent.com/pod-product-compliance
Lightning Source LLC
LaVergne TN
LVHW011320290626
842226LV00043B/1139

* 9 7 8 1 9 6 3 8 7 4 8 4 6 *